Your Five Senses and Your Sixth Sense

Taste

Connor Dayton

PowerKiDS
press.

New York

Published in 2014 by The Rosen Publishing Group, Inc.
29 East 21st Street, New York, NY 10010

First Edition

Editor: Jennifer Way
Book Design: Kate Vlachos

Photo Credits: Cover Jose Luis Pelaez Inc/Blend Images/Getty Images; p. 4 D. Hammonds/Shutterstock.com; p. 7 Dan Kosmayer/Shutterstock.com; p. 8 © iStockphoto.com/Chris Bernard; p. 11 © iStockphoto.com/Donna Coleman; pp. 12, 24 (salty) Lynn Watson/Shutterstock.com; pp. 15, 24 (food)w Ryan McVay/Lifesize/Getty Images; p. 16 AE Pictures Inc./Taxi/Getty Images; p. 19 iStockphoto/Thinkstock; p. 20 Altrendo Images/Altrendo/Getty Images; pp. 23, 24 (tongue) BestPhotoStudio/Shutterstock.com.

Library of Congress Cataloging-in-Publication Data

Dayton, Connor, author.
  Taste / by Connor Dayton. — First edition.
      pages cm. — (Your five senses and your sixth sense)
  Includes index.
  ISBN 978-1-4777-2856-7 (library binding) — ISBN 978-1-4777-2949-6 (pbk.) —
ISBN 978-1-4777-3026-3 (6-pack)
  1. Taste—Juvenile literature. I. Title.
  QP456.D39 2014
  612.8′7—dc23

                              2013016786

Manufactured in the United States of America

CPSIA Compliance Information: Batch # W14PK3: For Further Information contact Rosen Publishing, New York, New York at 1-800-237-9932

CONTENTS

4

Taste is one of your five senses.
You taste with your **tongue**.

Your tongue has bumps. These bumps contain taste buds.

7

8

Taste buds die off after 10 to 14 days. New taste buds grow in their place.

Some people have a very good sense of taste. They are called supertasters.

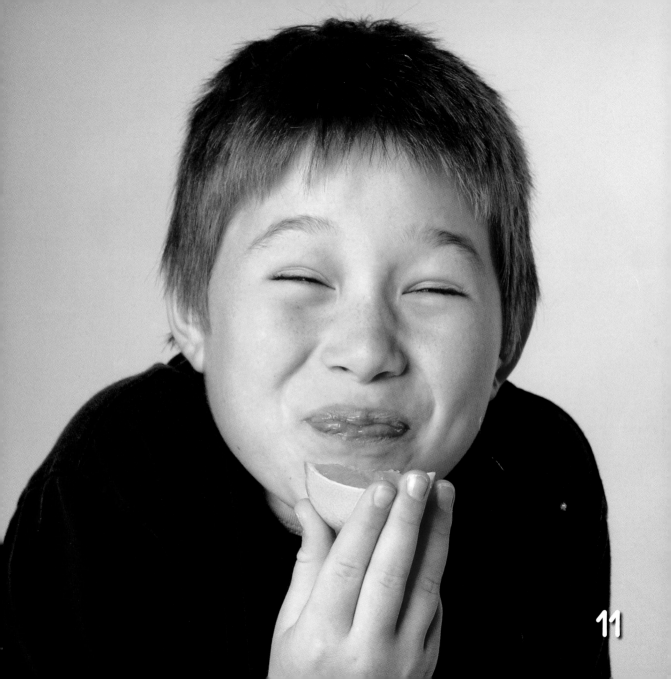

11

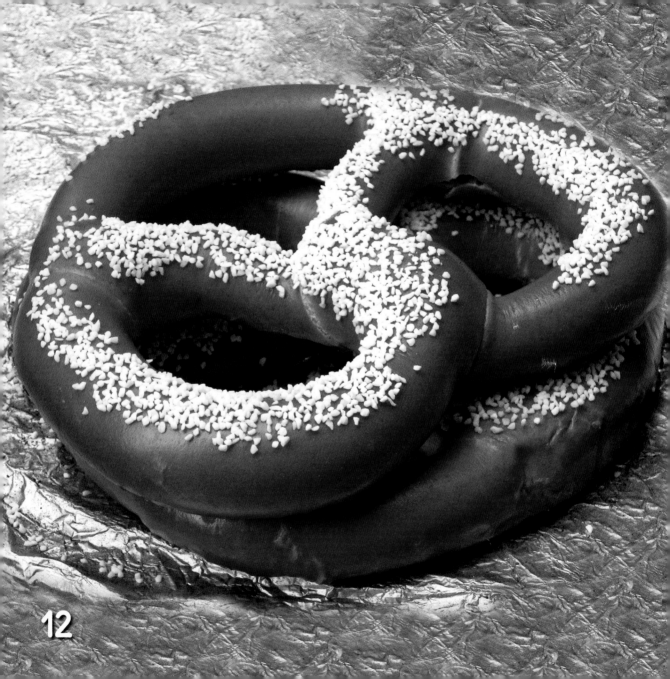

12

Sweet, sour, bitter, **salty**, and umami are the five basic tastes.

There are just a few tastes,
but there are many flavors.
Each **food** has its own flavor.

15

Taste buds have nerves.
Nerves send messages to
your brain.

The senses of smell and taste work together. It is hard to taste when you have a cold.

19

Your sense of taste can warn you. It tells you if food has gone bad.

You taste things every day.
What have you tasted today?

22

23

WORDS TO KNOW

food

salty

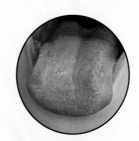
tongue

WEBSITES

Due to the changing nature of Internet links, PowerKids Press has developed an online list of websites related to the subject of this book. This site is updated regularly. Please use this link to access the list:

www.powerkidslinks.com/yfsyss/taste/

INDEX